Jes

The road to Jerusalem was dusty and it was a long way to walk.

A few miles from the city Jesus called two of his friends to him. "In the village over there you will find a young donkey which has never been ridden. Untie it and bring it here. And if anyone asks you what you are doing, say, 'The Master needs it.'"

The disciples were surprised. How could Jesus know this? But they did it just the same. And there was the colt! They brought it to Jesus.

Meanwhile, some of the people in Jerusalem were very excited. They had heard that Jesus might be coming to visit and now he was on his way! They felt sure he was going to perform some wonderful miracles. He might even chase the Roman army away.

That was what lots of people were hoping for – they were fed up with being ruled by soldiers from another country.

"Jesus is coming, Jesus is coming!" shouted a little girl.

Everyone rushed to look. They could see him in the distance, with his friends, moving steadily towards the city gates.

Some people grabbed branches off the trees to wave at him. Others took off their cloaks to make a soft carpet for the donkey to walk on. They shouted, they cheered, they clapped their hands.

"Jesus is our King! God bless the King!" yelled everyone.

When they reached the city Jesus went into the Temple. As Jesus stepped into the Temple courtyard, he looked around him in dismay. The place was full of stalls selling birds and small animals as offerings for the Passover festival. There were food counters and tables piled high with bags of Temple money.

"This place should be a place of prayer!"
said Jesus. "But you are cheating the poor.
You have turned God's house into a den of
thieves!"

Then Jesus was so cross with the traders that he tipped some of the tables over.

"That's going to upset a few people," whispered a little boy who had seen what had happened. "Those traders make a lot of money in here... they're not going to like Jesus one little bit!"

But Jesus didn't seem to care what people thought about him. He just wanted to tell them all about God, and how much he loved each one of them. He wanted to show them a new way to live.